GREAT MINECRAFT® BUILDS

YOUR UNOFFICIAL GUIDE TO BUILDING COOL MINECRAFT® TOWNS

S. D. MORISON

Enslow PUBLISHING

Please visit our website, www.enslow.com. For a free color catalog of all our high-quality books, call toll free 1-800-398-2504 or fax 1-877-980-4454.

Library of Congress Cataloging-in-Publication Data
Names: Morison, S. D., author.
Title: Your unofficial guide to building cool Minecraft® towns / S.D. Morison.
Description: New York : Enslow Publishing, 2023. | Series: Great Minecraft builds | Includes index.
Identifiers: LCCN 2022005771 (print) | LCCN 2022005772 (ebook) | ISBN 9781978529441 (library binding) | ISBN 9781978529427 (paperback) | ISBN 9781978529434 (set) | ISBN 9781978529458 (ebook)
Subjects: LCSH: Minecraft (Game)–Juvenile literature. | Cities and towns–Juvenile literature.
Classification: LCC GV1469.35.M535 M674 2023 (print) | LCC GV1469.35.M535 (ebook) | DDC 794.8/5–dc23/eng/20220209
LC record available at https://lccn.loc.gov/2022005771
LC ebook record available at https://lccn.loc.gov/2022005772

Published in 2023 by
Enslow Publishing
29 E. 21st Street
New York, NY 10010

Portions of this work were originally authored by Eric Tower and published as *The Unofficial Guide to Building Towns in Minecraft*. All new material this edition authored by S. D. Morison.

Designer: Rachel Rising
Editor: Jill Keppeler
Illustrator: Matías Lapegüe

Photo credits: Cover, pp. 1-4, 6, 8, 10, 12, 14, 16, 18, 20, 22-24 Orange Sky ART/Shutterstock.com; Cover, pp. 1-24 Phoenix 1319/Shutterstock.com; Cover, pp. 1, 3, 6, 8, 10, 12, 14, 16, 18, 20, 22-24 Soloma/Shutterstock.com; p. 4 bonandbon/Shutterstock.com; pp. 6, 8, 10, 12, 14, 16, 18, 20 Phoenix 1319/Shutterstock.com; p. 17 Wangkun Jia/Shutterstock.com.

Printed in the United States of America

CPSIA compliance information: Batch #CSENS23: For further information contact Enslow Publishing, New York, New York, at 1-800-398-2504.

CONTENTS

Words in the glossary appear in **bold** type the first time they are used in the text.

SETTLING DOWN

When early humans first began to stay in one place, building homes and creating communities, it marked a huge change in human history. It meant they could save their **energy** and **resources** instead of moving all the time. They could plant crops and raise animals so they didn't have to worry about finding food.

Settling down in one place in your *Minecraft* game may not change the world, but it can help you in similar ways. It means you'll have a place to keep your stuff, to raise crops and animals, and to build a life.

In the real world, it takes a lot of different people to plan and create a town. They include civil **engineers**, city planners, and many more people.

PLANNING AND BUILDING

The first part of planning a town in *Minecraft* will be picking a site. There are a few things to keep in mind. You might want to choose a site close to your **spawn** point. You may want to **explore** a bit first.

If you have a compass, it will lead you back to your spawn point. That's one reason to build nearby. There's a way to change this, but it will take a lot of effort and resources if you're playing in survival mode. In this mode, you have to collect all your resources yourself.

ADVENTURE MODE

You can make a *Minecraft* compass with four iron ingots, or bricks, and one piece of redstone dust.

A town should be near resources including water and trees. You may need to clear some space. This would be easier in creative mode than in survival mode.

BY THE BIOME

Minecraft worlds can be very diverse. There are many **biomes** that all have different resources including trees, animal mobs, and other features. For example, desert biomes have a lot of sand and cacti. Plains biomes are mostly flat. There aren't many trees, but horses can spawn there.

You may want to base your town around a natural *Minecraft* village. Villages are different depending on which biome they're in. Desert villages have lots of sandstone. **Taiga** villages (often in the middle of many spruce trees) have buildings made of spruce logs.

ADVENTURE MODE

Villages are the only places where the mobs called villagers spawn. However, you can cause villagers to spawn in other places if you're playing in creative mode.

Some *Minecraft* biomes have more hills and mountains than others. You can still build there, but it may take more work.

A SPOT OF SAFETY

Early humans started building communities and towns in part because there is safety in numbers. Wild animals and enemies were less likely to attack if there were many people living together. A *Minecraft* town can be a spot of safety as well. Sturdy buildings with doors can give villagers (and players) a place to go away from mobs and monsters

Make sure your town has lots of light sources, such as torches, lanterns, and campfires. Monsters such as creepers and zombies will spawn when it's dark out!

ADVENTURE MODE

If you're playing *Minecraft* in survival mode on the hard setting, remember that zombies can break down wooden doors. If you have a bed, however, you can sleep safely through the night.

You may want to build a wall around your town. Strong walls, iron doors, and lots of lighting will keep things safer.

WITHIN THE WALLS

What do you need or want within your *Minecraft* town's walls? Think about what you'd want in a real town. You'd want sources of water and food. You'd want a home where you can sleep at night and store your stuff. You'd want places where other people could live and work too.

You'll want these things in a *Minecraft* town as well. You can plant crops such as wheat, carrots, and potatoes to give you a food source. You can keep animals such as chickens and cows for eggs, milk, and meat.

ADVENTURE MODE

You can use crops to draw livestock into your *Minecraft* town. Wheat will draw cows and sheep. You can use potatoes or carrots to draw pigs. Seeds will draw chickens.

Minecraft crops need light and water to grow. How will you **design** your farm?

FIRE AND WATER

Towns in the real world need good building practices to keep them safe from fire—and they need firefighters if a fire starts anyway! You can avoid fires by building with stone and using lightning rods (made of three copper ingots) to draw lightning away during thunderstorms.

It's good to have a water source handy to put out fires too. You can create a simple well that never runs out of water. Dig a one-block-deep hole that's two blocks square. Fill two buckets with water and dump one each in two opposite corners of this hole.

ADVENTURE MODE

Buildings made of strong **materials** are also good to have if creepers get into your town! Each material has a different blast resistance, which is how well it will stand up to an **explosion**. Stone is stronger than wood.

Fire is a real-world danger, but the real world doesn't have monsters like giant spiders to attack your town! You can put overhangs on walls to keep them out.

A PLACE TO STAY

Of course, you need buildings in your town. If you're building in or around a naturally spawned village, you'll have a bunch to start with. Sometimes you can find **abandoned** villages in *Minecraft*. You can clean these up and use the buildings and resources for whatever you want. You'll have to remove a lot of spiderwebs, though!

Your own base should be the first thing you build. Then you can keep your bed, tools, and supplies there while you work on other things. You can always make it bigger or fancier later.

ADVENTURE MODE

Villagers can open wooden doors—even the door to your house! If you want them to stay out, use an iron door. You'll need buttons inside and outside to open it.

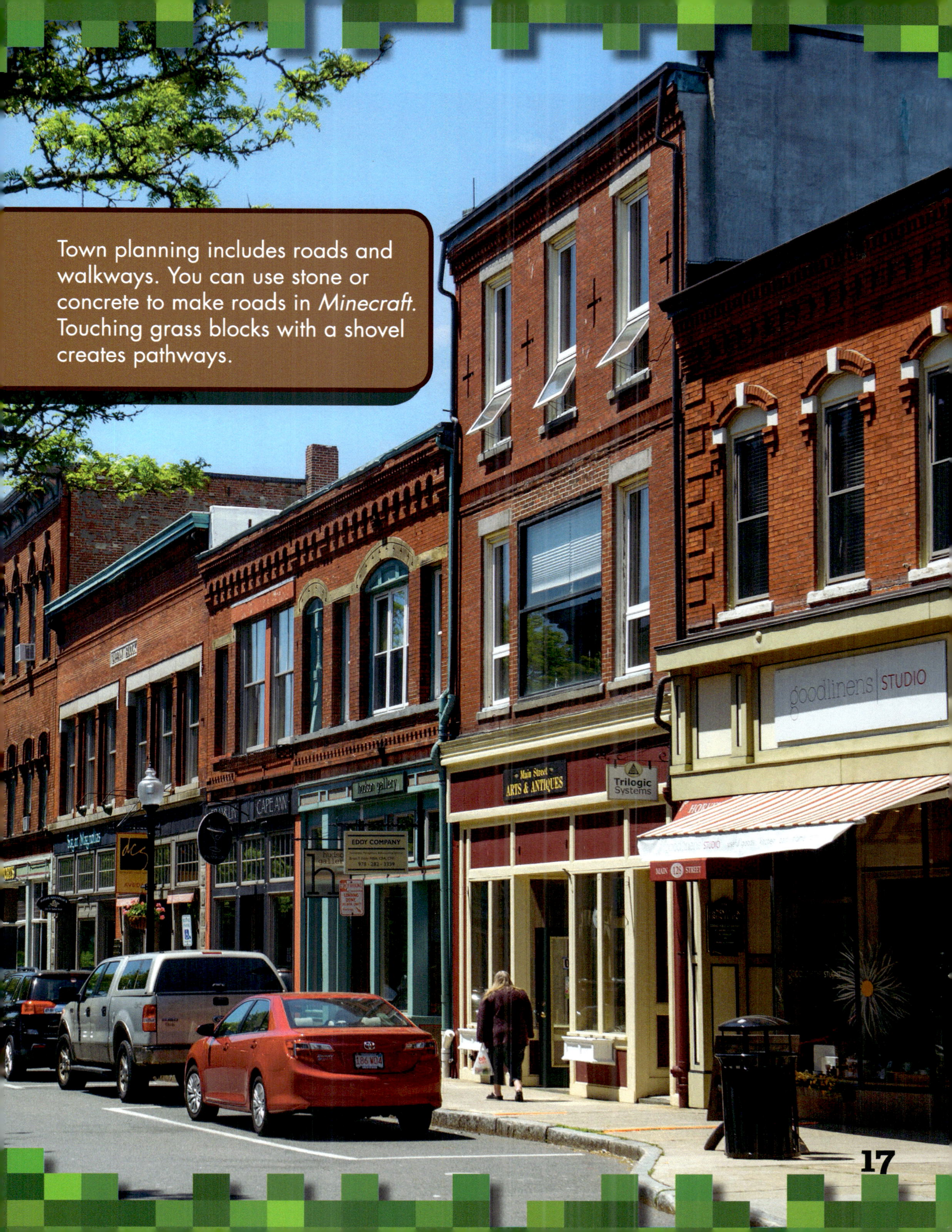

Town planning includes roads and walkways. You can use stone or concrete to make roads in *Minecraft*. Touching grass blocks with a shovel creates pathways.

A GROWING COMMUNITY

If you're growing a natural *Minecraft* village into a town, you may want to add more villagers. Different villagers have different jobs, and they can trade you for different items. New villagers appear first as baby villagers that grow up in about 20 minutes of game time.

For villagers to produce baby villagers, your town needs housing for them. Each villager must have a bed available. They also need plenty of food. You can toss food items such as bread or carrots at villagers to increase their supply.

ADVENTURE MODE

Baby villagers will chase each other around villages. They will go in and out of houses and jump on beds!

1

2

3

You can make lots of houses so you have room for more villagers. Make sure each house has a door and at least one bed. The image labeled 1 is the base. Images 2 to 5 stack on top of it.

4

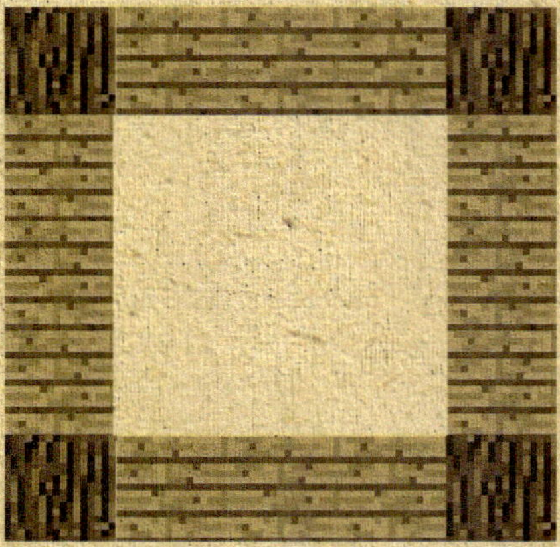

5

JOBS IN YOUR TOWN

In real life, lots of **variety** makes for a more interesting town. This is true in *Minecraft* too. There are more than a dozen different kinds of villagers. They'll look different depending on their jobs and what biome they live in. Their work area will look different as well.

Each villager job has a different job site block that must be present. For example, a farmer needs a composter, a fisherman needs a barrel, and a butcher needs a smoker. See if you can build a town with all kinds of villagers!

ADVENTURE MODE

As baby villagers grow up, they'll take on a job if there's an unclaimed job site block for it. If you add those blocks to your town, you can control their jobs.

Every building in your *Minecraft* town can look different. They don't need to be the same. Try new things and new materials.

GLOSSARY

abandoned Left by the owner.
biome A natural community of plants and animals, such as a forest or desert.
design To create the pattern or shape of something. Also, the pattern or shape of something.
energy The ability to be active.
engineer A person who works in engineering, or the use of science and math to build better objects.
explore To travel through a place to learn more about it.
explosion A sudden release of energy.
material Matter from which something is made.
resource Something that can be used.
spawn In a video game, to appear or cause something to appear.
taiga A biome that's generally cold and has many spruce trees.
variety Having many different things.

FOR MORE INFORMATION

BOOKS

Feroze, Jen. *How Cities Work*. Oakland, California: Lonely Planet Global, 2016.

Guthals, Sarah. *Building a Minecraft City: Build Like a Pro*. Hoboken, New Jersey: John Wiley & Sons Inc, 2018.

Zimmerman, Karla. *The Cities Book*. Victoria, Australia: Lonely Planet Global, 2018.

WEBSITES

Amazing Minecraft City and Town Builds
minecraftbuildinginc.com/6-amazing-minecraft-city-and-town-builds/
This website has inspiration for your town in examples of what other builders have created.

Simple Build Ideas to Grow Your *Minecraft* Town
www.sportskeeda.com/minecraft/5-simple-build-ideas-grow-minecraft-town
Done building the basics? This guide shows buildings you might want to create next.

Tutorials/Settlement Guide
minecraft.fandom.com/wiki/Tutorials/Settlement_guide
The *Minecraft* wiki offers ideas about creating a town, village, or city in the game.

INDEX